natural disasters

FIRST RESPONSE: BY SEA

Aileen Weintraub

HIGH
interest
books

Children's Press®
A Division of Scholastic Inc.
New York / Toronto / London / Auckland / Sydney
Mexico City / New Delhi / Hong Kong
Danbury, Connecticut

Book Design: Erica Clendening

Contributing Editor: Jennifer Silate

Photo Credits: Cover © U.S. Navy/Photographer's Mate First Class Brien Aho; p. 4 © Bay Ismoyo/AFP/Getty Images, Inc.; p. 7 © Gabriel R. Piper/U.S. Navy/Getty Images, Inc.; p. 8 © Library of Congress, Prints and Photographs Division, Washington, D.C.; p. 11 © William Vandivert/Time Life Pictures/Getty Images, Inc.; p. 12 © Central Press/Getty Images, Inc.; p. 14 Archive/Getty Images; p. 15 © U.S. Navy/Chief Journalist Dave Fliesen; p. 16 Robert Giroux/Getty Images, Inc.; p. 19 © Chris Hondros/Getty Images, Inc.; p. 21 © U.S. Navy/Photographer's Mate Third Class Rebecca J. Moat; p. 24 © U.S. Navy/Photographer's Mate Third Class Danielle M. Sosa; p. 27 © U.S. Navy/ Photographer's Mate First Class Bart A. Bauer; p. 30 © U.S. Navy/Photographer's Mate Second Class Timothy Smith; p. 32 © Mario Tama/Getty Images, Inc.; p. 34 © Ian S. Elias/U.S. Navy/Getty Images, Inc.; p. 36 © Mike Hvozda/U.S. Coast Guard/Getty Images; p. 40 © U.S. Coast Guard/Public Affairs Specialist Third Class Robert Nash.

Library of Congress Cataloging-in-Publication Data

Weintraub, Aileen, 1973–
    First response : by sea / Aileen Weintraub.
    p. cm. — (Natural disasters)
    Includes index.
    ISBN-10: 0-531-12434-7 (lib. bdg.)   0-531-18720-9 (pbk.)
    ISBN-13: 978-0-531-12434-5 (lib. bdg.)   978-0-531-18720-3 (pbk.)
    1. Lifesaving—Juvenile literature. 2. Lifeboat service—Juvenile literature. 3. Rescue work —Juvenile literature. I. Title. II. Series: Natural disasters (Children's Press)

VK1445.W45 2006
363.12'3581-dc22

                                                    2006011894

CONTENTS

Some victims of the Indian Ocean tsunami comb through the wreckage while others observe what is left of the city of Banda Aceh.

INTRODUCTION

One of the deadliest disasters in modern times struck Southeast Asia on December 26, 2004. Early that morning, a powerful earthquake rumbled at the bottom of the Indian Ocean. It was the second strongest earthquake ever recorded. The earthquake moved millions of gallons of water which rolled across the ocean in giant waves—a tsunami. The tsunami moved with the speed of an airplane. Most of the people living near the Indian Ocean had no idea that their lives were in danger.

The first place the tsunami hit was Banda Aceh, Sumatra. Some waves that hit Banda Aceh were 50 feet (15 meters) high. The waves moved quickly over the beaches and destroyed everything in their path. The water crumbled hospitals, homes, trees, and cars. The tsunami caused horrible damage in Indonesia, Sri Lanka, South India, and Thailand. Even those in countries as far away as Africa felt the effects of the giant waves. More than 200,000 people were killed. Millions were left homeless. Those who survived were without food, freshwater, or medical supplies. They needed help in order to stay alive.

Immediately after the tsunami, people took boats into the flooded areas to rescue people who had climbed up into trees and on top of buildings to escape the waves. Relief organizations from around the world jumped into action. There was little time to waste. Victims needed food, clean water, shelter, and medicine. Many people were seriously injured.

Planes and helicopters brought in supplies, but the people of Indonesia needed more than could be carried in by air. The United States Coast Guard and Navy sent large ships to Indonesia. These ships brought hundreds of tons of food, water, and supplies. One ship, the USNS *Mercy*, was a floating hospital. *Mercy* carried not only supplies, but also beds for patients, advanced medical equipment, and surgeons to help the injured. The coast guard and navy did whatever they could to help save the lives of thousands of people in need.

The USNS *Mercy* is a hospital ship and does not carry any weapons. Firing on the *Mercy* is considered to be a war crime.

A response by sea can be needed to save people from the water or to send supplies and other help long distances. Sea responders are always prepared to do what is necessary when a natural disaster strikes. Let's take a closer look at the jobs they do to help those in need.

The U.S. Coast Guard used posters like this one to recruit young men for duty during World War I (1914–1918).

chapter 1

A HISTORY OF SAVING LIVES

The organization in the United States that performs the most sea-based rescues is the U.S. Coast Guard. The coast guard started as the Revenue Marine Division of the Treasury Department in 1790. The Revenue Marine Division patrolled U.S. waters in cutters, vessels used to enforce laws, to make sure that people were paying taxes on goods they traded. It was formed to save money, not people, as the coast guard does today. The first water-based lifesaving services were not started by the U.S. government.

In the early 1800s, the Massachusetts Humane Society started the first volunteer lifesaving service. The Humane Society realized that only small rescue boats could save lives in a storm. A smaller lifeboat could be launched easily and not be in danger of getting stuck in shallow waters. They set up the first lifeboat station at Cohasset, Massachusetts, in 1807.

In 1848, the federal government started a system of lifesaving stations of its own to help sailors after shipwrecks. The Revenue Marine Division oversaw the lifesaving stations. Lifesaving stations were built up and down the coastline of the eastern United States. The stations had rescue boats and other supplies needed to save people and cargo from shipwrecks. The lifesaving stations relied heavily on local volunteers to help in recovery efforts after a shipwreck.

Unfortunately, no one was in charge of these stations and it usually took a long time to get the volunteers to the site of a shipwreck. Lives were often lost.

DID YOU KNOW?

In 1976, the coast guard became the first branch of the military to accept women into its academy.

Officers stand duty on the deck of a U.S. Coast Guard patrol boat.

MAJOR CHANGES

In 1871, Sumner Increase Kimball was named chief of the Treasury Department's Revenue Marine Division. Kimball immediately sent someone to inspect the lifesaving stations up and down the coast. He quickly learned that the equipment at the stations was rusty and in bad condition. He also discovered that the station volunteers were not well trained.

Kimball convinced the government to give the division money to make important changes. He used the money to replace the old equipment. He also hired six-man crews for all of the stations. Each of the crew members had to train thoroughly and follow a strict set of rules to insure quick, safe rescues.

A LIFE-SAVING SERVICE

In 1878, the U.S. Life-Saving Service was created as a separate agency under the direction of the U.S. Department of Treasury. Kimball became the general superintendent of the new organization. He remained the head of the service for almost forty years until finally retiring in 1915.

During that time, the Life-Saving Service grew rapidly. More than 170,000 people were saved by its crew members.

Following Kimball's retirement in 1915, Congress combined the U.S. Life-Saving Service and the Revenue Marine Division, by then renamed the Revenue Cutter Service, to create the U.S. Coast Guard.

Since its creation, the coast guard has been called upon to help in various emergencies around the world.

THE SINKING OF THE TITANIC

In 1912, the *Titanic* sunk after hitting an iceberg in the Atlantic Ocean. When the ship first began to sink, its crew members shot emergency flares into the night sky. Passing ships thought that the flares were firecrackers from a celebration. No one helped, and as a result hundreds of people died unnecessarily.

In the years that followed, changes in safety practices were made as a result of this event. The U.S. Coast Guard and coast guards from many other nations continue to make yearly

This drawing shows the sinking of the Titanic. The drawing appeared in the Illustrated London News in 1912.

iceberg patrols. They check to see where icebergs are in order to warn vessels.

AMVER, short for Automated Mutual Assistance Vessel Rescue system, was started in 1958. Ships can communicate easily with this system's radio waves and satellite technology to help those in trouble. They can also easily track and find vessels in need. Today, AMVER is used by boats from nations around the world.

Crewmembers get ready to launch an inflatable boat aboard a U.S. Coast Guard cutter.

The New York City Police Department's Harbor Unit cruises the waters of the Hudson River.

chapter 2

WHEN HELP CANNOT WAIT

When a disaster strikes, an immediate response is needed. Disasters on the water often require a special response. Frequently, whoever is nearest to an emergency at sea will respond first. In times of distress, the coast guard, local fire and police departments, and other military and even private organizations will lend a helping hand.

WATER POLICE

Many cities have water police units. They are usually part of a larger police force. For example, the water police of New York City, are known as the Harbor Unit. This division of the police department is responsible for patrolling New York's waterways. The Harbor Unit looks for crime and enforces laws relating to water traffic. They also conduct search-and-rescue operations. Most water police units are equipped with small watercrafts, inflatable boats, and large ships. Many of these boats have firefighting equipment and first aid kits onboard. When an emergency happens on the water, these units are often the first on the scene. The water police help in all sorts of situations, including floods and boating accidents.

GUARDING OUR NATION'S COASTS

The coast guard patrols the waters of the United States. The coast guard is broken up into two areas, the Pacific and the Atlantic. The areas are separated into districts. Each district monitors a part of the coastline of the United States and its territories.

The coast guard has many responsibilities in addition to performing search-and-rescue operations. It is a part of the Department of Homeland Security and, as such, must patrol the waters to maintain the country's security. It also enforces maritime laws, laws that govern actions on the water, and responds to environmental threats, such as oil spills. These duties keep the thirty thousand men and

On February 25, 2003, the U.S. Coast Guard became part of the Department of Homeland Security.

women of the coast guard very busy.

The coast guard can be called upon in many different types of situations. Its members are among the best-trained first responders–people who are called immediately to the scene of an emergency–in the world. The coast guard monitors channel 16 on VHF (very high frequency) radio, a device boaters use to communicate. This channel is reserved for emergencies. When a boat or ship sends out a "Mayday," or distress call, the coast guard is listening. The coast guard communicates with the people onboard the ship that is in trouble, in order to find out what kind of help is needed. Depending on the type of emergency, the coast guard may send a rescue boat or a helicopter to help.

DID YOU KNOW?

The coast guard is responsible for patrolling 95,000 miles (152,888 km) of coastline.

The coast guard also works with other organizations to help in times of disaster. It may work with local fire and police departments, other branches of the military, or different organizations around the world.

MILITARY HELP

The coast guard may be the branch of the military most used for rescue by sea, but it is

Three naval officers test an inflatable boat a short distance from the USNS *Mercy*.

21

BEAR IN ACTION

The Bear Search and Rescue Foundation was named after a dog named Bear. Bear helped search for survivors after terrorists knocked down the World Trade Center towers on September 11, 2001.

When Hurricane Katrina hit the Gulf Coast in August 2005, the Bear Search and Rescue Foundation sent twenty-seven teams of first responders. These teams were all made up of people that the foundation had either funded or trained. The teams rescued almost six thousand stranded people using boats and boat crews that the foundation provided.

not the only one. The air force, navy, army, National Guard, and the marine corps are all called upon for rescues by sea. Most often, such rescues are performed during combat, but these units are also called upon to help during natural disasters and other emergencies. The coast guard works mostly with the navy. In fact, the navy had rescue swimmers, people who drop from a helicopter into the water to help others, before the coast guard. The coast guard used the navy rescue swimmer program as a model for its own.

There are other rescue organizations in the United States that can be called upon to aid those in need of help on the sea. The Bear Search and Rescue Foundation helps search-and-rescue teams across the country. The foundation specializes in marine rescue training. They pay or arrange for instruction for first responders. They also provide free transportation for search-and-rescue teams to missions and training sessions. These teams work side by side with the local and federal search-and-rescue teams in times of crisis.

A navy instructor demonstrates rescue techniques for trainees at a San Diego naval station.

chapter 3

THE SEA RESPONSE

All first responders must be highly trained at their jobs. During an emergency, there is no room for mistakes. First responders put themselves in very dangerous situations in order to help others. Because of this, first responders must be trained to do their jobs in extreme conditions so that they will be able to help in any situation.

First responders often work long hours with no rest. In addition, first responders who work on the water have to be able to swim while carrying an injured person. All must be able to help a person until a hospital or doctor can be reached. Their training includes learning CPR (cardiopulmonary resuscitation) and other necessary first aid techniques. Some first responders are even trained to perform first aid while in the water.

SPECIAL TRAINING

The coast guard and navy have training academies for members. They learn all they need to know about being in the service while at these academies. Members who will work in search-and-rescue operations get specialized training. They learn first aid and how to operate the boats and helicopters used in rescue missions.

Rescue swimmers get further training than other members of the service. Coast guard rescue swimmers attend a special four-month training school. They must pass many physical tests and be able to work in rough seas for 30 minutes at a time. The training is so tough that more than half of those who enter the school never finish. After their training, they are ready to help in almost any disaster.

THE INDIAN OCEAN TSUNAMI

On that fateful day in December of 2004, when an earthquake created a powerful tsunami in the Indian Ocean, hundreds of thousands of people in eleven countries were killed. The tsunami waves swept away almost everything in their paths, including people, homes, and

A U.S. Navy landing craft air cushion vehicle (top) arrives off the coast of the tsunami-ravaged city of Meulaboh, Sumatra, with much-needed supplies.

hospitals. The millions of people who survived were left without shelter, food, or water. Many were seriously injured with no one to care for them.

Organizations from around the world sent rescue workers to help after the tsunami. The donations that poured in after the tsunami resulted in one of the largest international relief efforts in world history. Within hours of the tsunami, U.S. Coast Guard and Navy ships were headed toward the disaster site.

THE SHIPS ARRIVE

In total, the United States sent more than twenty-five ships to Southeast Asia. These ships were filled with equipment, supplies, and first

DID YOU KNOW?

Fishermen whose boats had not been destroyed used them to rescue stranded survivors after the tsunami. One group of fishermen saved more than five hundred people who were stranded on a large rock off the coast of India.

responders who were ready to help wherever they were needed. Only days after the tsunami, the U.S. Navy aircraft carrier *Abraham Lincoln*, which had been stationed in nearby Guam, arrived in Indonesia. It had picked up tons of desperately needed supplies on its way there. The large ship also brought sixteen helicopters that would be used in relief missions.

When the *Abraham Lincoln* arrived in the area, its crew members moved the supplies onto the helicopters. The helicopters were flown to the affected areas and dropped the supplies to those in need. This ship also had another very important job. It took seawater and processed it into over 400,000 gallons (1,514,164 liters) of fresh drinking water per day. Men on the ship even stopped taking showers so that the people of Indonesia could get as much freshwater as possible.

WITH MERCY

Another ship that rushed to the area was the USNS *Mercy*. The *Mercy* is a hospital ship. The ship has twelve operating rooms, advanced medical equipment, a pharmacy,

The **USS** *Abraham Lincoln,* a navy supercarrier, assists the **USNS** *Mercy* with the Indonesian relief effort.

and one thousand hospital beds. So many hospitals were destroyed in the tsunami that the USNS *Mercy* was badly needed. In the days and weeks following the tsunami, the services and supplies brought to the area by navy and coast guard vessels helped thousands of people.

Less than one year later, many of these ships would be called upon again to help for another natural disaster. This time, the disaster struck at home, in the United States.

HELPING OUT AT HOME

On August 29, 2005, Hurricane Katrina slammed into the Gulf Coast of the United States. Hurricane Katrina was a very powerful hurricane. It brought heavy rains and high winds to the coasts of Louisiana, Mississippi, and Alabama. The hurricane's strong winds swept the waters along the coast of the Gulf of Mexico inland. This flooding and the high winds of the hurricane destroyed many cities and towns along the coast. The levees, walls built to hold back floodwaters around New Orleans, Louisiana, broke in some places. Water quickly filled the streets of the city. Many people died. Houses were destroyed. Thousands of people were stranded on their rooftops. Pipes that had carried clean water broke. More people would die if help did not arrive soon. First responders came by sea, air, and land to help.

SEARCH AND RESCUE

The coast guard sent 111 small boats, including rigid inflatable boats and motor boats.

31

A coast guard rescue boat looks for survivors of Hurricane Katrina in the flooded city of New Orleans.

Additionally they sent thirty cutters–large boats over 65 feet (20 m) in length–to the Gulf of Mexico to help. More than five thousand members of the coast guard traveled to New Orleans to help. Members of the air force, navy, marine corps, National Guard, and many rescue organizations rushed to New Orleans.

One of the first priorities was to rescue those who were stranded on building rooftops in the flooded city. Many rescue workers used small lifeboats. Small boats can move on the water quickly and easily. In the aftermath of Hurricane Katrina, small boats were used to patrol the flooded streets in search of survivors.

Helicopters also flew above the city to help with the search. Many people had been swept away in the rising floodwaters. Some clung to trees or debris to stay afloat. Rescue helicopters dropped rescue swimmers to help lift the people from the water to safety. The coast guard alone saved more than twenty-four thousand lives by boat and helicopter.

BRINGING IN THE BIG SHIPS

For the response by sea, the United States government also sent hospital ships to the areas in need. The two hospital ships were the USNS *Mercy* and the USNS *Comfort.* The USNS *Comfort* was sent to Mississippi with 122.5 tons (111 metric tons) of supplies onboard. The hospital ship was loaded with three million dollars worth of medical supplies. It also had

The hospital ship USNS *Comfort* stops in Florida to load up supplies on its way to lend aid in the Gulf Coast.

570 people onboard to help with relief efforts. They included teams of doctors and nurses.

Other large ships brought much-needed fuel to the devastated areas. All of the gas stations had been shut down after the hurricane. The relief workers needed fuel to get from place to place. It would be impossible to save people without ambulances, fire trucks, and other vehicles.

COMMUNICATION

Being able to communicate is also very important during times of disaster. The coast guard lost much of its communications equipment during the hurricane. VHF towers, which were used for radio and television broadcasts, were damaged and not working. Most Internet and phone lines were also not working. The coast guard brought in special mobile communication towers to help them keep in touch with the many boats and helicopters they had in the area. The coast guard did such a good job of staying organized in the face of this terrible disaster that one of its leaders, Vice Admiral Thad Allen, was named commander of the New Orleans relief effort.

ANSWERING THE CALL

After Hurricane Katrina and the Indian Ocean tsunami, first responders by sea were there to answer the call for help. Without that help, many lives might not have been saved.

New Defender-class boats, such as this one patrolling New York Harbor, will help the **U.S. Coast Guard** face future security and rescue challenges.

chapter 4

LOOKING TOWARD THE FUTURE

After Hurricane Katrina, the coast guard and many other rescue organizations realized that they had to make some changes to be better prepared for natural disasters. One of the major problems the coast guard had during the hurricane relief effort was with communications.

After Hurricane Katrina, the coast guard approved a new emergency communication system. This system, called Rescue 21, will make it easier for the coast guard to communicate with other boaters and its own vessels. With Rescue 21, the coast guard will no longer be dependent upon old VHF communication systems. Instead, it will use a digital communication system with a larger range and clearer signal. It will also use six different emergency channels instead of the one currently available, allowing rescuers to talk to more than one person in need at a time. Rescue 21 also uses advanced technology that allows the coast guard to trace the calls it receives so that it can accurately locate boats in trouble.

GETTING BIGGER AND BETTER

Another major issue facing the coast guard is its very size. With only 39,000 people in the service, the coast guard is the smallest branch of the military. It has a big job to do and not a lot of people to do it. After Hurricane Katrina struck, almost one-third of all its members were deployed to the affected area. That meant there were fewer people to help in emergencies elsewhere. Certain law enforcement activities were stopped altogether while the coast guard was at work in the Gulf. Currently, the coast guard is working to increase the number of members it has (as well as upgrading their training) so that it will be able to meet future needs. The number of people joining the coast guard is slowly and steadily increasing.

NEW BOATS

In addition to more people, the coast guard is also getting more boats. Among these boats are the National Security Cutter and the

Defender-class boats. The National Security Cutter is much larger than a regular cutter at 419 feet (127 m) long. It can stay out to sea for sixty days and is equipped with the Rescue 21 system as well as many other technologies.

The Defender-class boats have already replaced many older boats in the coast guard's fleet. These 25-foot (8 m) long boats can be used for many different missions, including search-and-rescue, security patrols, and more. The Defender-class boats have special foam collars to keep them afloat. Older boats used inflatable collars, which could be ripped or torn. Many rescue organizations today are using boats with foam collars for their by-sea response fleet.

First responders by sea work in difficult conditions, and they face danger every day. As rescue operations grow, more people will be needed to do this important job. With better boats, continued training, and new technology, sea responders will be ready for the next disaster.

A coast guard homeland security boat cuts the waves during a routine training exercise.

WHAT DO YOU DO?

The best way to help a first responder is by staying safe in an emergency. Below are some basic things you can do to prepare for a disaster.

- In the event of a disaster, call for help as soon as possible. Every second counts.

- Prepare a plan for you and your family for different types of disaster. Know where your family will go in case of emergency.

- If it is raining heavily, listen to the radio or TV for flood warnings.

- Make sure that you have an emergency kit ready just in case. You should have canned food, water, a first aid kit, a flashlight, a battery-operated radio, and extra batteries.

NEW WORDS

academy (uh-**kad**-uh-mee) school that teaches special subjects

AMVER (**am**-vur) the Automated Mutual Assistance Vessel Rescue system used to help ships from all nations communicate with and find one another

CPR (**see pee ar**) Cardiopulmonary Resuscitation; a method of reviving people using mouth-to-mouth breathing and rhythmical compressing of the chest

cutter (**kuht**-ur) ship used to enforce laws; today they are ships 65 feet (20 m) long or larger used by the U.S. Coast Guard

devastation (**dev**-uh-stay-shuhn) complete destruction

earthquake (**urth**-kwayk) sudden, violent shaking, caused by shifting of Earth's crust

first responder (**furst** ri-**spond**-ur) person called upon to help immediately after an emergency has happened

flood (**fluhd**) when water overflows beyond its normal limits

hurricane (**hur**-uh-kane) violent storm with high winds that starts in the areas of the Atlantic Basin near the equator and then travels north, northeast, or northwest

NEW WORDS

levee (**lev**-ee) bank built up near water to prevent flooding

lifeboat (**life**-boht) a strong boat usually carried on a larger ship that is used to save lives during shipwrecks or other emergencies

lifesaving station (**life**-sayv-ing **stay**-shuhn) place where lifeboats and other equipment are kept to be used during an emergency

rescue swimmer (**ress**-kyoo **swim**-mer) person specially trained to be dropped from a helicopter in order to save others in trouble in the water.

Revenue Cutter Service (**rev**-uh-noo **kuht**-ur **sur**-viss) an organization started in 1790 to patrol the waters of the United States in order to enforce tax laws

satellite (**sat**-uh-lite) a spacecraft that is sent into orbit around Earth; many have communication equipment onboard that sends and receives signals from Earth

tsunami (tsoo-**nah**-mee) very large, destructive series of waves caused by an underwater earthquake or volcano

VHF (**vee aych eff**) stands for very high frequency, a frequency of radio waves used by people at sea to communicate

FOR FURTHER READING

Miller, Debra. *Hurricane Katrina: Devastation on the Gulf Coast.* Detroit, MI: Thomson Gale, 2006.

Roza, Greg. *Careers in the Coast Guard's Search and Rescue Unit.* New York: Rosen Publishing Group, 2003.

Stone, Lynn. *Coast Guard Cutters.* Vera Beach, FL: Rourke Publishing, 2005.

Thompson, Tamara. *Emergency Response.* Detroit, MI: Thomson Gale, 2004.

Torres, John A. *Disaster in the Indian Ocean: Tsunami 2004.* Newark, DE: Mitchell Lane Publishers, 2005.

RESOURCES

ORGANIZATIONS

Historian's Office
U.S. Coast Guard Headquarters
2100 Second Street, SW
Washington, DC 20593-0001
Phone: (202) 267-1394
http://www.uscg.mil/hq/g-cp/history/
  collect.html

Pacific Tsunami Museum
130 Kamehameha Avenue
Hilo, HI 96721
Phone: (808) 935-0926
http://www.tsunami.org

United States Navy
Chief of Information
ATTN: Department of the Navy
1200 Navy Pentagon, Room 4B463
Washington, DC 20350-1200
http://www.navy.mil

RESOURCES

WEB SITES

Bear Search and Rescue
http://www.bearsearchandrescue.org
Check out this site and learn more about the history of this organization and its important activities.

Time for Kids: Hurricane Katrina
http://www.timeforkids.com/TFK/katrina
Read stories from kids who survived Katrina and who are helping survivors on this informative Web site.

United States Coast Guard
http://www.uscg.mil
Learn more about the many different missions of the Coast Guard, its history, and the new additions to the fleet on this Web site.

INDEX

INDEX

ABOUT THE AUTHOR

Aileen Weintraub is a freelance author and editor living in the scenic Hudson Valley in upstate New York. She has authored over forty-five books for children and young adults. She writes for a variety of newspapers, magazines, and newsletters and edits historical manuscripts.